Recycling

Paper

Kate Walker

MACMILLAN
LIBRARY

First published in 2009 by
MACMILLAN EDUCATION AUSTRALIA PTY LTD
15–19 Claremont Street, South Yarra 3141

Visit our website at www.macmillan.com.au or go directly to www.macmillanlibrary.com.au

Associated companies and representatives throughout the world.

National Library of Australia
Cataloguing-in-Publication data

Walker, Kate, 1950 (Jan. 10)-
    Paper / Kate Walker.
    MYL : Recycling

    Includes index.
    For primary school aged children.
    ISBN: 978 1 4202 6609 2 (hbk.)

    Recycling (Waste, etc.) – Juvenile literature.
    Waste minimization – Juvenile literature.
    Waste paper – Recycling – Juvenile literature.
    Paper – Juvenile literature.

363.7282

Edited by Julia Carlomagno
Text and cover design by Christine Deering
Page layout by Christine Deering
Photo research by Legend Images
Illustrations by Gaston Vanzet

Printed in China

Acknowledgements
The author and the publisher are grateful to the following for permission to reproduce copyright material:

Front cover photograph: Boy and girl recycling paper, photo by Stockbyte/Getty Images

Photos courtesy of: © Lourens Smak/Alamy, **13** left; Coo-ee Picture Library, **15**, **18** bottom left and bottom right; David Porter
School, **28**, **29**; © Hotduckz/Dreamstime.com, **30** centre; © swq/Fotolia.com, **30** top; Dev Carr/Getty Images, **14**; Photodisc/
Getty Images, **12** right; RL Productions/Getty Images, **4**; David Silverman/Getty Images, **12** centre; Stockbyte/Getty Images, **1**;
© Missing35mm/iStockphoto.com, **30** bottom; © Greg Nicholas/iStockphoto.com, **18** top; © Ralph125/iStockphoto, **5**; © 2008
Jupiterimages, **17**; MEA Photo, **3**, **22**; © Peter E. Smith, Natural Sciences Image Library, **12** left, **16**; PaperlinX Office, **13** right;
Photolibrary/Randy Faris, **6**; Photolibrary/David R Frazier, **9** all; Photolibrary/Elfi Kluck, **21**; Shutterstock, **7**; © Dana Bartekoske/
Shutterstock, **26**; © Countryroad/Shutterstock, **23**; © Les Scholz/Shutterstock, **20**; © Annamaria Szilagyi/Shutterstock, **8**;
Copyright 2006 Yellow Woods Challenge UK, **27**.

While every care has been taken to trace and acknowledge copyright, the publisher tenders their apologies for any accidental
infringement where copyright has proved untraceable. Where the attempt has been unsuccessful, the publisher welcomes
information that would redress the situation.

Contents

Glossary words

When a word is printed in **bold**, you can look up its meaning in the Glossary on page 31.

What is recycling?

Recycling is collecting used products and making them into new products. Recycling is easy and keeps the environment clean and healthy.

Every piece of paper that is recycled saves resources and helps the environment.

Why recycle paper?

Recycling paper helps:

- save **natural resources** for future use
- reduce **pollution** in the environment
- keep waste material out of **landfill**.

If more paper was recycled, landfills such as this could be closed.

Paper products

People use many different paper products every day. Paper is used in:

- paper towels
- tissues
- carry bags
- toilet rolls
- cardboard boxes.

Paper towels can be used to wipe up mess.

Even though many people use computers, most people still use a lot of paper. Paper is used in:

- note paper and envelopes
- books
- newspapers
- magazines.

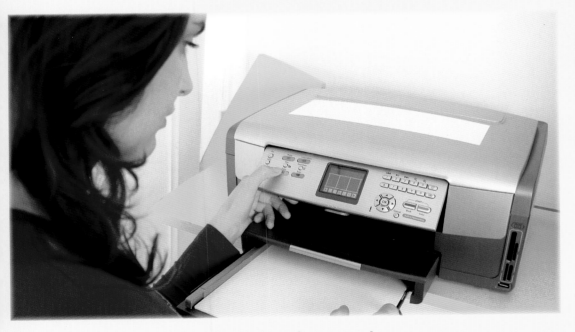

Many people use paper to print documents.

How paper is made

Paper is made from wood, which comes from trees. Trees are a natural resource that can be replaced. However, trees are now being cut down faster than new ones can grow.

Trees are cut down to be made into paper.

The paper-making process

Wood goes through a three-stage **process** called **pulping** to make paper.

Stage 1
Wood is shredded into wood chips.

Stage 2
Wood chips are mixed with water and chemicals to make paper pulp.

Stage 3
Wet paper pulp is dried in thin, flat sheets.

Wasting paper or recycling paper?

Wasting paper uses natural resources, increases pollution and adds to waste.

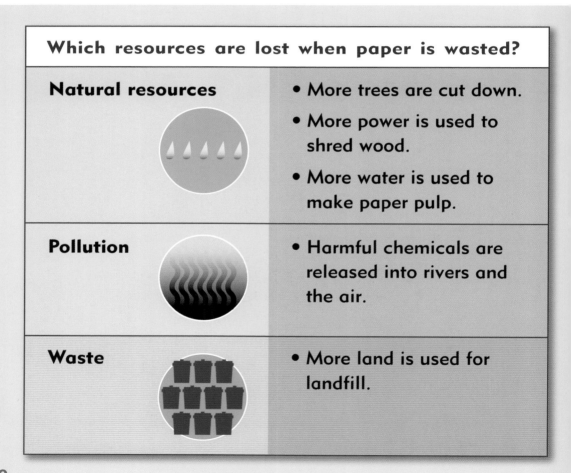

Which resources are lost when paper is wasted?

Natural resources
- More trees are cut down.
- More power is used to shred wood.
- More water is used to make paper pulp.

Pollution
- Harmful chemicals are released into rivers and the air.

Waste
- More land is used for landfill.

Recycling paper saves natural resources, reduces pollution and cuts down waste. Which do you think is better, wasting or recycling paper?

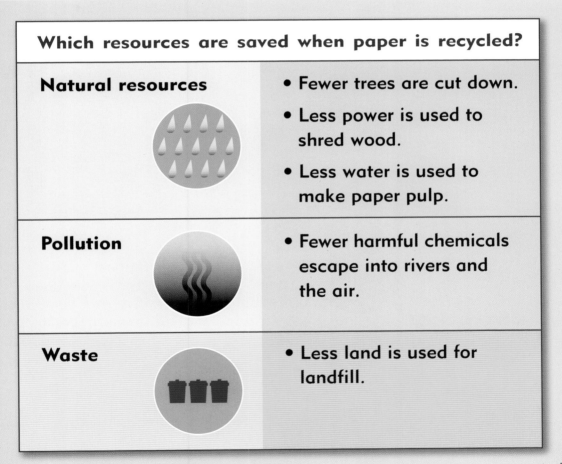

Which resources are saved when paper is recycled?

Natural resources	• Fewer trees are cut down. • Less power is used to shred wood. • Less water is used to make paper pulp.
Pollution	• Fewer harmful chemicals escape into rivers and the air.
Waste	• Less land is used for landfill.

How paper is recycled

Paper is recycled through a five-stage process. This process begins when we recycle used paper and it ends with new paper products.

Stage 1
Used paper is collected from recycling bins left on the curbside.

Stage 2
Different types of paper are separated into **pure streams**.

Stage 3
Paper is shredded and mixed with water to make paper pulp. Chemicals are added to the paper pulp to remove ink and glue.

Stage 4
Recycled paper pulp is added to new paper pulp.

Stage 5
Paper pulp is made into new paper products.

Recycling paper at home

Most households in towns and cities have special recycling bins. All **recyclable** paper and cardboard can be put into these bins.

Paper is put into recycling bins, which will be emptied by recycling collection trucks.

How to recycle paper

The correct way to recycle paper is:

- keep paper dry
- remove any metal clips, except staples
- keep plastic bags out of recycling bins.

Remove metal clips from paper before recycling it.

Recycling paper at school

Schools use paper for lesson sheets, notes and craft activities. Most classrooms have a paper-recycling bin. A team of **monitors** looks after the bin.

A classroom recycling bin should be placed where it can easily be seen and reached.

Paper-recycling monitors

Paper-recycling monitors:

- take turns to empty the recycling bin
- remind classmates to keep recycling paper
- check that only recyclable paper has gone into the recycling bin.

These paper-recycling monitors are responsible for checking that newspapers get recycled.

Can all paper be recycled?

Not all paper can be recycled. Paper coated with wax or plastic is **non-recyclable**. Removing wax and plastic from paper costs too much.

Fluorescent paper, food-stained paper and paper coated in wax or plastic should go in the bin for general rubbish.

Paper **contaminated** with food or oil is also non-recyclable. Food and oil cause problems in the paper-pulping process.

Which types of paper are recyclable?	
Recyclable paper	**Non-recyclable paper**
✔ white printer paper	✖ plastic-coated paper
✔ newspapers	✖ wax-coated cardboard
✔ envelopes	✖ fluorescent paper
✔ egg cartons	✖ food-soiled paper or cardboard, such as pizza boxes
✔ cardboard	✖ tissues

Is recycling paper the best option?

Recycling paper saves trees and helps the environment. However, recycling paper also uses resources. A lot of water is used to turn recycled paper into paper pulp.

Recycling paper uses water, which is a valuable natural resource.

Trucks that collect paper for recycling burn **fossil fuels** in their engines. Burning fossil fuels causes air pollution.

Paper-recycling trucks burn fossil fuels, which causes air pollution.

Reducing and reusing paper

There are many ways to reduce paper use and reuse paper. One way is to write on both sides of every sheet.

An easy way to reduce paper use is to use every sheet of paper twice.

Some simple ways to reuse paper are:

- cut scrap paper in half and staple together to make notepads
- recycle old cards to create new hand-made cards
- use envelopes more than once.

Pictures from used birthday and Christmas cards can be used to create new cards.

Make a box town

Some foods come in cardboard boxes. Build a town using food boxes of different shapes and sizes.

What you need:
- different-sized food boxes
- cardboard tubes of different lengths
- paints
- marker pen
- scissors
- glue.

What to do:

1 **Paint the boxes different colours.**

2 **Draw doors and windows on the boxes with a marker pen.**

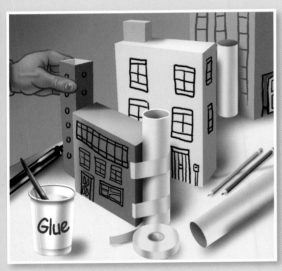

3 Glue cardboard tubes to some boxes to make chimneys.

4 Arrange the boxes to form a town. Cut out tree-top shapes and glue them to cardboard tubes to make trees.

25

School recycling projects

In the United Kingdom, many schools collect old Yellow Pages telephone directories for recycling. The paper is recycled into animal bedding, egg cartons, cardboard and newsprint.

Old directories are replaced each year with new books and updated telephone numbers.

Schools that collect the highest number of Yellow Pages directories win cash prizes. Some students use the telephone directories to make giant sculptures before the books are recycled.

Milton Junior School students made this owl sculpture from old Yellow Pages directories.

Cozy Comfort Pillows and Critters

Students at David Porter School in the United States are prize-winning **recyclers**. They won a Super Recyclers Award for their Cozy Comfort Pillows.

Students at David Porter School made Cozy Comfort Pillows with used paper.

Students used shredded classroom paper to stuff their hand-decorated pillows. They also made doorway draft stoppers with used paper.

David Porter School students made draft stoppers, called Cozy Comfort Critters, with used paper.

How recycling paper helps animals

Paper is made from trees. Cutting down trees destroys animal **habitats**. When you recycle paper you save the habitats of many animals, such as:

- koalas

- tree snakes

- owls.

Glossary

contaminated	ruined by small amounts of harmful material
fossil fuels	oil-based fuels that power engines in cars and trucks
habitats	areas where animals live, feed and breed
landfill	large holes in the ground where waste material is buried
monitors	school students who are given special duties
natural resources	materials found in nature that people use and value
non-recyclable	not able to be recycled
pollution	waste that damages the air, water or land
process	a series of actions that bring about a change
pulping	a process that turns wood chips, water and chemicals into paper pulp
pure streams	groups of items made of the same material
recyclable	able to be recycled
recyclers	people who recycle

Index